Everything We Always Knew Was True

Also by James Galvin

James Galvin

Everything We Always Knew Was True

COPPER CANYON PRESS

PORT TOWNSEND, WASHINGTON

Copper Canyon Press is in residence at Fort Worden State Park in Port Townsend, Washington, under the auspices of Centrum. Centrum is a gathering place for artists and creative thinkers from around the world, students of all ages and backgrounds, and audiences seeking extraordinary cultural enrichment.

LIBRARY OF CONGRESS CATALOGING-IN-PUBLICATION DATA

Names: Galvin, James, author.
Title: Everything we always knew was true / James Galvin.
Description: Port Townsend, Washington : Copper Canyon Press, [2016]
Identifiers: LCCN 2015039063 | ISBN 9781556594922 (softcover)
Classification: LCC PS3557.A444 A6 2016 | DDC 811/.54—dc23
LC record available at http://lccn.loc.gov/2015039063

98765432 FIRST PRINTING

Copper Canyon Press
Post Office Box 271
Port Townsend, Washington 98368
www.coppercanyonpress.org

Acknowledgments

Thanks to the magazines in which these poems first appeared:

The American Poetry Review, Arroyo Literary Review, The Columbia Review, Connotation Press: An Online Artifact, Free Verse, The Iowa Review, Lana Turner, The Literary Review, The Missouri Review, Narrative, The New Yorker, Poetry, and *The Threepenny Review.*

"On the Sadness of Wedding Dresses" also appeared in *The Best American Poetry 2015.*

Contents

Everything We Always Knew Was True

Natura Morta

—for Craig Arnold

I

I don't mind one or two
Turkey buzzards spooling
Over my head in a famously
Heart-torn Western sky.
It doesn't mean anything.
They're just doing their job.
They aren't complaining, either.

I don't mind a dozen or so
Such birds cruising over a carcass
Like teenagers round a Dairy Queen.
They're just out to get some.
That is all it means.

II

But at the BBQ
On Independence Day
2008,
When Craig played guitar,
And everybody sang,
When all we were doing was toasting
The dregs of our freedom, saying
Good-bye to our Constitution,
Hundreds of buzzards, maybe thousands,

Frenzy-flocked over Beth's yard,
A black blizzard of rancid
Plumes—I don't know what
It meant, but it meant something.

III

My lady draws flowers for hours and hours—
Pistils and stamens, stems and veins,
Paintbrush, wild iris, sage leaves and phlox—
Black ink shines from her pen
Or the finest available sable tip.
Sometimes she mixes feathers and flowers,
Birds and blossoms, transforming forms
Into swift fragile lines, colors and fragrances
Stroked into irrefutable black.

She captures motion with motion,
Stops it cold—irises dying,
Hummingbirds hovering, all
In breathtaking cuttlefish code.
She never draws buzzards so far as I know.

IV

Then I'm out fixing fence, tightening
And splicing the snow-broke wires.
I pull off the road into the sage and flowers,
And the fragrance under my tires explodes
Into the still summer air.
I think of her sketchbook that burgeons and blossoms
Into a black blizzard when she closes it.

Roadside Ditch *Natura Morta*

No one can draw fast enough
To capture the cut
Iris before its form falls
From its former self.

But when we passed a patch
In the ditch,
She told me to stop and she stepped
Down, opening her clasp
Knife. She spared one iris
With an impressionistic
Cocoon on its stem
And cut the flower beside it.

Once home
She rendered in a careful hurry.
She drew into the night as the iris died.
I woke grafted to her
In a vague, translucent hammock of dread.

A Thousand and One Avatars

It appeared like a bullet hole
In the day-lit stratosphere
That leaked a bright
White light.
Then it began
To approach us
Where we stood next
To the open palm
Of a lake.
It whirled to the north
And came down
Like a comet's tail,
Then like a cloud of frost,
Slowly lofting,
A fuzzy galactic avatar.
Then we could tell it was birds,
Wings set, hovering
And flipping like pages
Of news in wind.
Then it was
White pelicans
With nine-foot wingspans,
And we saw the black-tipped
Remiges
Of the largest of boreal birds
Coming to rest
On our modest lake
In their ordained sortie
From Florida, the Gulf Coast,

And Panama,
To their home in British Columbia.
It was a pod,
Then a squadron,
Then a scoop,
As their wings became parachutes,
And they water-skied in.
There must have been a thousand of them,
Veering and banking
To avoid collisions.
Some luffed,
Waiting their turn.
It took an hour
For them all to come down
And fold their wings
And huddle in the middle
Like a melting ice floe.
They bore spikes for beaks,
And their necks hooked
Like shepherds' crooks.
And then I thought
Of the blind man
I'd seen in the market
In a small village
In Italy,
Where this sort of thing can occur,
His open palm of bills,
All folded and tucked
Like origami,
Creased in different shapes
(Someone must have done this
For him),

Triangles, rectangles, squares,
So he could tell their
Denominations.
A door opened,
And a wind scattered his currency.
All the people knelt
To gather his geometries
And return them
To his hand.

Snow

It was snowing nurses.
The blond ones
From ICU.
They wore those perky
Little nurse hats,
White coats.
They wore surgical
Masks and carried
IV needles
And bags of morphine.
They had sponges
In their pockets.
They landed gently
On the lawn,
And looked around,
Not knowing
What to do.

It was snowing
Polar bears,
Who loved us for
Our temporary mercy.
They landed gently
On the lawn,
On all fours,
But then stood
On their hind legs
And sniffed all around,
Confused.

It was snowing sawdust
From the Amish coffin shop.

It was snowing shuttlecocks
That looked like pastries
Or tiny volcanoes.
At least they looked at home
Lying on the grass.

It was snowing pastries.
It was snowing swaddled babies.
They landed gently.
It was snowing wan
Corpses in dress whites
That had started out
As babies with zero
Knowledge of pastries,
Or shuttlecocks,
Or sawdust,
Or polar bears,
And had (fate
Being fatal) of nurses,
Now, no knowledge
Or need.

Bringing Down the House

When they tore down the auditorium
The facade went first, rebar snarling out like a
Nest of centipedes. When they tore down
The auditorium, excavators
And backhoes roamed like sci-fi mantises,
Munching with hydraulic jaws as they
Hunted and gathered and devoured. When they
Tore down the auditorium, percussive
Wrecking balls kept time
As I thought of years of arts performing magics.
I saw Baryshnikov twice. Heard Pavarotti,
Marsalis, and Ma, heard Bobby McFerrin, Bernstein,
The Kronos Quartet. The stage was a realm of light,
Sound, and dance. Applause came in tsunamis.
All in Iowa City, Iowa.
Then came the real flood. Mud took the stage,
Mold took a curtain call. They tore down the
Auditorium, but I remember.
Wynton Marsalis gave a master class
To three or four Iowa high school white-bread
Jazz combos. When Marsalis walked in they throttled
Their horns and saxophones, and who could blame them?
They jammed. He taught them to listen to one another
And respond. "Did you hear that B-flat I played?
Well why didn't you do something about it?"
And, "You can't get up on a stage then act
Like you don't belong there." He took questions. They had
A few shy ones. Then one girl, whose parents
Probably couldn't afford that night's performance,

Asked the best question ever: "Will you
Play something for us?" By way of answer
He laid down an impossible Dizzy Gillespie
Riff. A stunned silence forestalled the applause,
A silence such as that which overawes
The din of tearing down the auditorium.

The Newlywed Acrobats

—after Chagall

Even though he is in church, the groom's long yellow hair lilts in a
slight breeze from the sacristy.

He sports gold-sequined tights and
slippers.

The bride is decked out in a gold bikini.

Her breasts are
two miracles.

Her smile is, well, blinding.

He flips the wedding ring
high into the air like a florin.

She spears it (did you guess?) on her
ring finger.

The priest juggles chalices as they kiss.

The crowd
roars joyously as she cartwheels down the aisle.

The groom does
back-handsprings and sticks a double flip at the door.

On the steps,
an avalanche of confetti.

Clowns are shot from cannons to the
right and to the left.

On golden ropes the couple swings into the
waiting limo, which looks like a gold coffin being sawed in two and
appears to split in half as it disappears.

There happens to be a
trampoline in front of the hotel.

They spring each other higher and higher and scarily higher until he vaults into a fourth-floor window and she follows like a comet's tail.

The bridal suite is golden with smoke and mirrors everywhere.

A trapeze over the bed lolls back and forth.

So many options for the finale!

Too many!

A lifetime of diversion!

They look deeply into each other's eyes, his bleary, hers fierce with determination.

She says, "You're not gonna believe this part."

Belief

For most of us belief
Is the opposite
Of knowing.
Little is known
About Michelangelo
Merisi,
Detto Caravaggio.
In any room that has a Caravaggio
(The Vatican's
Art historian
Told me)
All the other paintings disappear.
We believe
He treated his canvases
With a powder
Made of dried
Fireflies
To create a photosensitive
Surface to paint on.
We believe he belonged
To a gang of swordsmen
Painters
Whose motto was "No hope:
No fear."
We believe he died of wounds
Sustained in a duel.
Or was it boring malaria?
Who cares.
Only the paintings matter.

The paintings of Caravaggio
Make all the other paintings disappear.

During the restoration of the Sistine Chapel
I stood on the scaffold
Under God's finger
Touching life into Adam.
"Go ahead," said the restorer,
"You can put your finger there."
I didn't dare.
When I asked the art historian
Who God was
Hanging off of,
So as to touch Adam
And not fall out of the sky,
He replied,
"God can't fall out of the sky.
We believe she is the uncreated Eve."
Hmm.

If I told you my daughter
Was baptized
In the Sistine Chapel,
The first child to be baptized there
In more than three hundred years,
You might not believe me.

I've seen the Pauline Chapel,
The Pope's private chapel,
The memento mori
Of Saint Lawrence's burnt and grinning head

(We believe as they were roasting him he said,
"You can turn me over now, I'm done on that side").
Can you believe it?
I've seen Saint Lucy's eyes.

If I told you I've seen
The vault Saint Peter's bones were hidden in,
A plumb-bob drop
From the top
Of Michelangelo's dome,
Right through the altar,
And way underground,
And the man in the crypt was carbon-dated spot on,
And missing his feet
(Remember he was crucified upside down).
Think about it.

Time doesn't change,
Nor do times.
Only things inside time change,
Things you will believe, and things you won't.

Cinque Terre

Time was the five towns
That share the sheer escarpment
Above the Mediterranean
(Leaning now forward,
Now away, like a schoolgirl who wants to kiss
But is too shy)
Were linked only by the sea.
I doubt if anyone *chose*
To live there
Until late in the last century.
The hardscrabblest place in Italy,
Vines and olive trees grow on terraces
Chiseled with pickaxes
Into volcanic cliffs—
Convict work turned over, over generations,
Into convictions.
Then they chipped a precarious path
That swoons between the towns
For local trade and gossip
(You can walk that path today).
There was always fishing
And the sea stayed indigo.
Then came the train
Tunneling the towns together—
A jailbreak to nowhere.
Then came the roads,
Dropped like rescue ropes from above.
Then came the rich, the tourists, sunbathers
From every elsewhere

Who flop on the beach near
The house Montale grew up in
"In crushing isolation."
The towns are like glacial moraines
Of stone houses
Stuck in the gullets of their declivities.
One teeters on a knoll above the sea.

This morning I'm watching the doings
In the harbor at Riomaggiore.
Young boys dangle strings with hooks
Among nonplussed
Schools of minnows—
Never any luck.
Older boys, sunbaked,
Try to impress their heartthrobs
With heart-stopping dead-drops
From a twenty-meter
Precipice into the azure water
Of their hometown harbor.
They fall faster than falling. They fall
Like arrows shot straight down
And surface grinning
And climb the cliff side
For another tilt at another fling.
I'll bet their ancestors never
Wooed that way,
The *contadini* who hacked
A life into the high terraces
Of their handmade Purgatory.
Fear, for them, was no bouquet.
From the tourist path,

Another path strikes straight up
Into an olive grove
Behind a hunched mesh gate
That skreeks in sea breeze.
A sign on the gate sings,
This is not a path,
As if that could be true.

What It's Like

A pebble dropped into a well to see
How far down the water is.
The report:
No way to say how deep.

Five Paintings by Clara Van Waning

—for Allan Gurganus

I only paint landscapes. People are just
Too sad. Sometimes I paint folks turning away,
Hiding their faces. Faces are too sad.
The loveliest are saddest, so says me.
That's why they turn away, ashamed. That's why
Fans and parasols are in demand.

I paint my own front yard. The big pole gate
Left open so the subject can become
The narrow two-track road, which turns away,
And vanishes. It could be coming home
Or going. I'm not telling. The open gate
Means someone left, and I am waiting for them

To come home. You have to tell the truth.
I have the perfect pastel color to show
How awful dry a year it's been this year.
If you lived here you'd know from the grass and the kind
Of yellow flowers that it's almost fall.
The sage is the same gray green it always is.

I have the perfect color to paint it hopeful,
But paint it plain as dirt, as true. My pictures
Aren't bad. Folks buy them. But they aren't
All that good either, since no one ever
Taught me. The two-track road just disappears
No matter how hard we work, how hard we pray.

When the fire started on George Creek, I painted it.
Who was George, I'd like to know, to have
A creek named after him? But never mind.
I painted ponderosas right up front
That looked just like the tree of smoke coming
At me over the ridge, but green. I couldn't

See any flames, so I didn't paint any.
George Creek is a wild place and hard to reach,
But I had just the right color to paint
The green swath of tall grass that leans over
The ridge to where the fire burned, the right
Color to paint the smoke leaning downwind,

Toward home. Trees are hard to paint and smoke
Is even harder. Sometimes I feel I'm hanging
On to the God-lit canvas, like a sail,
I feel the darkness behind me looking over
My shoulder. I feel that darkness swirling me backward
Into it. It's worse when I paint a lake

With peaks behind it. My secret is I paint
From a place that would have to be *on* the lake or in it,
And I don't have a boat. The mountains turn
Away. All my landscapes are sunrises.
People think that that's a good thing. Sun
Coming up, I mean. I have the perfect color

To color them in early light. It isn't
A good thing, but I paint it. There seem to be
Recurring themes of... I don't know. Well look

How plain I am, and where I live. I paint
A sunrise scene: a man rowing away
From a house with no lights on. It's on a jetty.

If you didn't know which lake it was, which house,
You might just think that he was almost home.
But I know that's a sunrise on the ridge,
And because the man is turned away, wearing
A long-billed cap (and I gave him red galluses),
And because of shadows under his sweeping oars,

And skittish shadows the prow makes in its wake,
He rows away from that dark house, for sure.
I'll just tell you one more painting. Sunrise
On sandstone cliffs is like the sky is bleeding
On the earth. There are Indian pictures on those rocks.
I know how to find them: stick men, maybe

Gods, with spears and shields. I have the perfect
Color for sunrise on red desert rocks.
Three mustangs are coming toward me from a pond.
The stallion is the subject of the painting.
He's standing close to me, but turned away.
He's worried that the others will not follow.

They will, but far away and slow. I have
All the colors I need for wild horses.

What It's Like

Horseback in an old burn.
Deadfall everywhere.
No way forward.
No way to turn around.

Bet

On the far side of the ridge at my back, the sky
Gasps and won't let go its breath. Over
Here the sky is smaller, manageable,
Imaginable. At my back over
That wave of ridge, the Laramie Basin swoops
Like a nighthawk, then rises again up to
The blue Medicine Bow under pure ether.
I can feel the cold of snowfields in my spine.
But here, under the smaller sky it's all
Watercolor strokes of green bleeding
Into each other. The ridge I'm looking at
Crests and falls under pines, like a breaker to
Its knees on a coast, which is a lighter, wobblier
Green of tall grass—a hayfield ready for mowing,
Itself more like an ocean than a shore.
Down its middle a drunken, willowy creek
Staggers. The air is heavy with willow scent
And pine duff. The heat is light. Down there, across
The meadow, in the shadow of the falling
Ridge (you wouldn't see them if I didn't
Tell you), two men, motionless, study
The last snowdrift. They lean on spades in waist-
High grass, wearing green hip boots. The snowdrift looks
Like a homeless man, lying, half-fetal with
A dirty sheet thrown over him. A month
Ago, when the bet was made, that drift looked more
Like a barn, and was bigger than one. Even then
It was the only white besides the clouds,
When there were clouds in the small sky among

All that green, and hanging on right where
The lodgepoles left it after a winter spent
Combing snow out of the wind and heaping
It at their feet like wealth. Pat and Lyle
Bet every year on whether that snowdrift
Will survive until the Fourth of July.
Pat is sixty-five, as old as Lyle
Will live to be. His eyes are dimly green.
Lyle's are laser blue. They eye the heap
Of snow. It's the slowest race in the world, and no
Money on it. They made their bets a month
Ago today. They are looking at it hard
In its shade of trees and the north side of its ridge.
"What's today?"
    "Today?—Today's the first."
"I don't think he will make it till the Fourth."
"I do. You betting against yourself?"
      "Are you?"
"Not yet. There's still a chance that he could make it
Till the Fourth, depending on cold nights."

On First Seeing a US Forest Service Aerial Photo
of Where I Live

All those poems I wrote
About living in the sky
Were wrong. I live on a leaf
Of a fern of frost growing
Up your bedroom window
In forty below.

I live on a needle of a branch
Of a cedar tree, hard-bitten,
Striving in six directions,
Rooted in rock, a cedar
Tree made of other trees,
Not cedar but fir,

Lodgepole, and blue spruce,
Arrogating like
Bacteria the fan-
Lip of a draw to draw
Water as soon as it slips
From the snowdrift's grip

And flows downward from
Branch to root—a tree
Running in reverse.
Or I live on a thorn on a trellis—
Trained, restrained, maybe
Cut back, to hold up

Those flowers I've only heard of
To whatever there is and isn't
Above.

Wildlife Management I

All the trees kept their own counsel without any wind to speak of, until one lone limber pine began gesticulating wildly, as if it suffered from its own inner cyclone.

It was like a lunatic in the courtroom of other trees.

We forgot about the sunset and the dark coming on across the plain.

Then the reason appeared: a mother antelope had twin newborns backed into the tree and fended off a pair of coyotes who darted in and feinted out, knowing she couldn't defend them both.

The girl I was with shrieked, "Do something!"

I thought of the rifle back at the house.

I thought of a litter of coyote whelps in a den somewhere nearby.

I thought of the three-hundred-yard sprint to the tree.

The mother antelope would be first to bolt, and those coyotes would have the aplomb to make off with both twins.

I said no.

The antelope struck out with her forelegs, she butted the coyotes back, until one of them got the chance they had orchestrated and caught a twin and trotted off, dangling it by the nape as gently as if it were her own.

Wildlife Management II

I woke from a bird hitting the window, almost, I thought, hard enough to break it.

The sun rose knowingly.

I slid the sash up and stuck my head out like someone in an Italian movie.

A flicker lay on its back—stunned—but it was blinking steady as a railroad crossing.

Was there misery to put out?

Would it come to its "senses"?

I thought where were you when bark beetles killed half my trees?

Then I remembered, sleepily, reading that flickers mostly eat ants.

I went back to sleep for half an hour, and dreamed, as I often do, of horses.

When next I looked, the bird still lay still, still blinking.

Maybe, I thought, it can't roll over.

So I went down and rolled it over.

Terrified by my touch, it came to life and flop-hopped down the hill into some sagebrush.

It didn't fly, but it didn't seem broken, either.

I tried to find it later.

No luck.

Whether
it lived and flew off, or died thrust into a bush, was, apparently,
none of my business.
If it were thrust into a bush, I knew the ants
wouldn't wait for the guest of honor to start dinner.

Wildlife Management III

Without the manifest necessity of a paint-laden brush, the motion traced by the painter's hand would mimic that moth's fragile desperation against the glass as it seeks escape into the already painted sunset.

It drops to the sill periodically the way the painter's hand would drop to the palette.

Then it sputters back up erratically and zigzags to indicate the horizontal nature of sunsets.

On the other side of the glass, free to the air, a nighthawk enacts the same erratic striving, up and up and down and sideways then up again and falteringly up until it drops, wings folded, suicidally earthward.

It spreads its wings just above the ground for the life-saving aerialist's breathtaking swoop.

Air through feathers (they call it drumming) hums like a wind harp or tissue paper on a comb.

The nighthawk flies like that, erratic as a bat, because that's how moths fly, and that's what nighthawks eat and what they feed their fledglings.

Nighthawks build no nests but lay their eggs on bare ground.

Their camouflage is so perfect you can find them only by accident.

If you are out walking and the mother flies up, pulling that clichéd broken-wing trick, and you mark the spot she rose from, you can find the eggs.

If you go back after they hatch, you can look right at them and think they aren't there—just some small chunks of wood.

So I'm watching this nighthawk and the moth on the glass in their painterly struggles that mirror each other as the sunset reclines, aloof.

This is the only moth I've seen this rainless summer.

The only nighthawk too.

So I open the window and give them both what they want.

Some Tree

The best time to view
The oldest ash tree
In Johnson County
(Now that we've cut it down)
Is a whiteout at night,
Like now,
When the porch light strives on
Against the hurrying,
Particulate, ineluctable assault.
Through the slant static
It appears to me
Lording it over summer,
The twisting, overreaching
Sultan
Of its surround,
Leaves tickled
On boughs
From branches as long
As the tree is tall,
Branches themselves
The size of big trees
Longing almost
Horizontally away.
How can they bear
Their own weight without breaking?
A thick yellow rope swing,
With a knot at the end,
Waits for the children,
And here they come shrill.

School's out
And they want to measure
The trunk's circumference.
How big is big?
They hold hands in a ring around it.
I took the rope down
When they grew up
And flew away.
And that was the first limb
To give up to the torque
Of its own impossibility,
The one the children swung from.
It whumped on the yard
And reached across the street,
Exposing a family of raccoons
That were living
In its hollow.
The tree was calling it quits.
Then another limb tore off
And pounded the neighbors' drive.
We took the tree down
And left the stump.
It was time.
A circle of arrowheads crowns
The ancient's last claim,
All nosing the two hundredth ring.
"That must have been some tree,"
Strangers say.

What It's Like

A freight elevator in free fall.
A grand piano in it.

A Sunday Morning in Humboldt County, California, Circa 1980

Under Stalin's unwieldy hammer
Only literature
That expressed a certain
"Mild optimism"
Was allowed.
Up here
On this black beach
Behind the Redwood Curtain,
Fog blubbers the shore.
I can barely see my bare feet
Skirting the tideline
Of humbled waves.
The ocean shushes,
But I can hear
Up ahead
In the blind air,
Someone playing a bassoon.
And there she is
In a black evening gown,
Seated, facing the sea,
In a black folding chair.
And why not?
The sand is the same black
As the bassoon.
From up on the highway overhead
The tires of an eighteen-wheeler
Loaded with redwood logs
Moan in harmony.
In town the church goners

Drone, too, but I can't hear them.
In fog like this the paddleboat enthusiasts
Stay home.
I miss them.
Maybe the bassoonist will see my tracks
When she rises to leave.
I can only hope.
What I share with her
In this fog
Are the deep-keeled sound of the bassoon
Under oceanic shushing,
The log truck's whining,
The imagined prayers
Of the prayers,
And the mild optimism
Of the redwood trees left standing.

The Hunchback

Today I am captive to a caustic loneliness,
A certain fear that the Future Stone Age

Approaches ineluctably like a fog
Bank moving inland, obliterating any

Particulars of trees, buildings, beliefs,
Not just effacing the world's most vulnerable

Details, but devouring them. I know
That out there in the fog, April's oak, ash,

And maple leaves are blindly striving, people's
Houses crumble while cradling intricacies

Of familial peculiarities.
Even the people who live them will have no

Idea of what they mean in their denials
And self-deceptions as they eat a piece of toast,

Dance barefoot in the grass, water the flowers,
Or turn the page of a novel in which a hunchback

Is spotted hiding in a corner of
An empty swimming pool. Soon it will all

Have turned into a nostalgic fairy tale,
A lie of culture and nature and the Future

Stone Age will arrive to whisper in each of our ears
Everything we always knew was true.

She Said It Was like Talking to a Post

When talking to a post
Imagine
That the post hears everything—
Every nuance,
Every innuendo.
You can't let your mind wander.
Try structuring an argument:
If, but, therefore, or
In the first place, the second place,
And so forth.
Talking to a post requires
Absolute attention;
Imagine
That the post is not a post.
The post is Heraclitus,
Hitler, or a fire hydrant.
If that doesn't work,
Remember
The post was once a pine tree
With greeny needles
That sang in thin wind
High on the snowy slopes
Of the Rocky Mountains.
Talking to a post
Is the hardest thing there is
Because
The post is talking to you
Beyond your understanding.

Another Fable

The old man, in his day, well let's just say
He took a lot of meat without a license.
That he was arrogant, well that just goes
Without saying, so we don't, but see,
He had a reason. He thought that a man
Who owned his land shouldn't have to pay to
Hunt. Not the government, especially.
So though he never, as some poachers do,
Hunted in the spring or summer, killing
Does with fawns out of sheer depravity
Or desperation or both (sometimes it's hard
To tell the difference, though, "There Are Roughly
Zones"). He never—it was a point of honor—
Hunted legally—not antelope
Or deer or elk. He never had a fishing
License either, for that matter, never.
No harm, really, except his son, before
He was old enough, himself, to learn to poach,
Was terrified each time the old man brought
A gutted carcass home and strung it up
In the toolshed with a pulley hooked to a stave
That cross-pierced slits behind Achilles tendons,
And put a Master padlock on the door,
And told his son the word was mum in case
The game warden came to snoop around. Remember
The son was very young and he still thought
That those who broke the law were put in jail,
That the whole family could go to jail
Since they knew, and would not tell, what hung

In the toolshed, behind the padlocked door.
It isn't imagery, the painterly,
I'm after here, but stale fear in a boy
Each time he opens the toolshed door, even
In spring or summer when there's no meat hung,
The smell of blood and the prey's adrenaline,
Which triggers in the boy a predatory
Inability to turn and run.

What It's Like

The kind of spider that spins by casting
Its threads into the wind.
The gossamer like a ghost tree on the high desert.
There's one between my window and the screen.
The branches are hollow,
Not sticky but slick
So the prey tumbles from branch to root
Where the spider waits.
Then comes a frost and the spider dies,
And the wind takes back what it made.

Isla de los Alcatraces

I wanted to understand Alcatraz.
I wanted to know the horror and despair
That ruled there. I took a boat. I took
The tour, headphones and all—narrated by
Prison guards and convicts. It didn't work.
All it was was interesting, which isn't.
I read two books about it, which helped me some,
But I never really contacted that hurt.
I was not unlike, perhaps, the window-licking
Snobs who show up at the end of this poem
To end it. On the wharf I looked at photos:
Mustachioed Confederates and local
Fans of slavery, not too worried;
A group portrait of renegade Indians
Posed in rows like a Paleo rugby team.
They hadn't done anything worse than try to go
Home, and shot back when they were shot at—
Desert folk who had never seen the sea,
Or a city, or boats. They'd never seen a camera,
So didn't know their souls were being stolen.
It didn't take them long to realize
That reservations about reservations
Paled when faced with The Rock. On docking one reads
The original welcome sign: *When you break the rules*
You go to prison. When you break the rules in prison
You go to Alcatraz. A Dantesque wink.
The headphone tour is a whitewash, and the cells,
Though tiny, are tidy, only one con per.
The headphones list escape attempts—how many

Men were shot or drowned or both. Just one
Made land, but was easy to collect. Just one
Escaped, which means they never found his body.
The tour doesn't tell you but books testify
That if you didn't carry a shiv you got stabbed,
And if you got caught with a shiv, you got the hole—
Round-the-clock darkness, water, and four slices
Of bread a day for up to forty days.
And days on Alcatraz were all there were—
No weeks or months or sentences for life.
You had to be a "daddy" or a "queen."
There was no in between, no opting out.
How can you sentence someone to sodomy?
We, the people, do it every day.
Both cons and prison guards agreed: the worst
Thing about Alcatraz was its drop-dead
View of the city. Not even Dante punished
Lifers with visions of the afterlife.
Most murders took place in the showers or in
The Recreation Yard as San Francisco looked
Away, aloof, a golden odalisque.
A favorite pastime of city socialites
Was sailing their yachts as near to The Rock as they dared.
The nearer the better. They thrilled to thoughts of thugs
Behind bars—"Scarface" Capone (who, in prison,
Became a skillful cobbler, according to the tour),
"Machine Gun" Kelly, "Creepy" Karpis. But
The lethal cons were not the superstars.
The scary guys were backward losers, psychos,
Guys with IQs smaller than their hat sizes,
Who'd never had a moll or limousine.
The Rock was more of a lethal loony bin

Than prison, and correction wasn't on
Anybody's mind. So sailing yachts
Around The Rock became a popular game.
If they drew too near some shots were fired from the tower,
In jest, to shoo the revelers away.
But from the Recreation Yard, if wind
Was right, inmates could hear the shallow banter,
The laughter of girls, the clinks of champagne toasts.
They could see the white outfits and jaunty caps
And sunglasses. They could see the perfect teeth.

Winter Scene: The Sign

It's a rite of passage, locally, to take the plunge from the bridge
into the dead-looking water, which is, in fact, replete with suck-
holes.

    The sign commemorating the last drowning's date is gone.

Someone took it for a souvenir.

           Now, under ice, the river is
running dark.

       If I said it is still I'd be lying.

             It is still.

               We know it
moves because it is the river, and we've seen, in summer, the
comatose fannings of carp.

       They do that to stay in one place.

Every now and then one rises to feed.

            You have to imagine them
but you know they are down there because, watching a patch of
open water from the leafless limbs of four oak trees on the bank,
four bald eagles hold still.

       Four certainties.

Why the Ocean Needs to Forget about Morris Louis

Something we never meant to say (or did we?)
Reified the glee club and made them glum.
The glum club hates you now, get used to it.
They're all morticians anyway, it's just—
Why did it have to be us to break the news
Of the word-spill, and what it did or didn't do
To the marsh and all of its inhabitants—
Storks, pious as parking meters, crabs,
Clumps of grass like monstrous, wavy tweezers,
Tortoises burdened by nobility?

The accident, or eventuality,
Will not go away, go back to torrents
Falling terrorized in rocky gorges
Choked with boulders big as wrecked boxcars
Spilling freight of clear and gleeful gushes
So cold they'd break the roof of your mouth like glass.
But down by the sea, confidence sets in
Again. The river is a tepid, silty
Lick that strikes the oily waves as interesting.

Simon Says,

You look like you could use a little sleep.
Simon Says, If you were lost in the woods
I would find you. Simon Says, It's time
For a new statement of purpose. Simon Says,
Make a decision based on consequence.
Simon Says, Now make the same decision
Based on moral law, no matter what
The consequences are. Then Simon Says,
The hoax is anagogical. No hooey.
Simon Says, It's the lollapalooza tree.
Simon Says, Your corpse is in perfect health.
Take your givens with a rain of salt.
Simon Says, We are dying for each other.
Simon Says, Please get me out of here.
Simon Says, I'll do anything you say.

Chain Saw Dreams

The extended family
Of restless chain saws
(The Stihls, the Husqvarnas)
Has the same collective
Dream every night.
Last week their dream came true.
The extended family
Of restless chain saws
Dreamed high wind,
And by morning there were broken trees
All over town—
A chain saw's life and heaven.
The extended family
Of restless chain saws
Did not rest.
They shrieked to life at dawn.
They did their worst.
They shrieked demonic
Shrieks of joy for days.
They outshrieked freight trains.
They outshrieked the interstate.
They outshrieked the memoirists
Who feature themselves
As victims.
Serious shrieking.
Chain saws—banshees with dreams
That sooner or later
Come true.
They remonstrate us

To lower our standards
While dreaming.
They want us to plant more trees
For them.

Thanksgiving on the Line

The Weatherman said, "Sunny statewide."
The Weatherman lied.
The Medicine Bow grated snow down
Without even a storm to work with.
The mountains enshrouded themselves in their task.
Or was it their cast?
Or why not just say
The sun spun itself like a grindstone,
And steel dust fell from a deep blue sky?
Who worked the treadle?
Who cut and trued the gritstone wheel?
I don't know about any of it.
Never any accumulation.

I know a wheel doesn't turn by itself.
My second guess is the wicked stepmother,
Having spanked the only child with a stick of firewood,
Swept the spilled sugar
Away but not up.
By and large,
I don't know about any of it.
I don't even have an opinion.
I am simply not familiar.
I'm just sawing off another day to length.
Sawdust drifts over my boots.
When a wind comes up
It's like cockroaches when the lights come on: Exeunt.
It should be winter, but the worst fire season ever still lingers.
Note to Smokey: Only forest fires can prevent forest fires.

The sawyer is gizzened.

The cast decitizenized.

To be a citizen, you need a storm to work with.

.

Giving Up the Ghosts

The address book I bought in Italy
Thirty or so years ago
Had a blue leather cover.
It got to where
All that held it together
Was duct tape and rubber bands.
Every time I opened it
Friends, dead and alive,
Fell out together.
My address book was deciduous.
My address book was a tree
Full of falling leaves,
Full of butterflies, dead and dying.

I bought a new address book
(Black plastic cover bound by metal rings)
And set about the tedium
Of transcribing.
There were more dead friends than I'd guessed,
And I thanked each one
For not making me write down
Their info.
And I thanked the ghosts—
Those names whose people
I couldn't remember.
"Who's that?"
And I tried to conjure them up,
Relieved when I couldn't.
I got on with the work

Of securing the living,
Giving them places, phone numbers,
Imagining each one alive and free.

On the Sadness of Wedding Dresses

On starless, windless nights like this
I imagine
I can hear the wedding dresses
Weeping in their closets,
Luminescent with hopeless longing,
Like hollow angels.
They know they will never be worn again.
Who wants them now,
After their one heroic day in the limelight?
Yet they glow with desire
In the darkness of closets.
A few lucky wedding dresses
Get worn by daughters—just once more,
Then back to the closet.
Most turn yellow over time,
Yellow from praying
For the moths to come
And carry them into the sky.
Where is your mother's wedding dress,
What closet?
Where is your grandmother's wedding dress?
What, gone?
Eventually they all disappear,
Who knows where.
Imagine a dump with a wedding dress on it.
I saw one wedding dress, hopeful at Goodwill.
But what sad story brought it there,
And what sad story will take it away?
Somewhere a closet is waiting for it.

The luckiest wedding dresses
Are those of wives
Betrayed by their husbands
A week after the wedding.
They are flung outside the double-wide,
Or the condo in Telluride,
And doused with gasoline.
They ride the candolescent flames,
Just smoke now,
Into a sky full of congratulations.

Take as Needed for Pain

—for Dan Beachy-Quick

As Arab Spring turns into Fall,
First frost zombies the grass
And Sibyl's leaves read what they said
And see where they didn't.
Thirtier than twenty-nine
She drove a nail into the spine
Of geography,
Where a light breeze pronounces
The curse of invulnerability.
Let me pause to give you an example:
There are never any vacancies.
The season's bilked,
Gallied to a standstill.
All the traitors wait for the dispatch.
How many unmarked graves will you be needing?
Queried the head snowflake.
Now that content is out of the way,
All manner of antics have at it.
There is no last stand, nor ever was.
And who doesn't want a nuke?
There's flukes, said Stubb, and lit his pipe.
Oh, Ahab.

Americanathon

Waiting for the New Ice Age to come along
Like a dawdling child from a previous eon,
Waiting for the homeless man to go on home
With his tired cardboard sign that says, *Anything helps*,
Waiting for a cure, waiting for the closeout sale,
The black sail, a new tarboosh and a tiny red car,
A new, improved, and safer war,
A harmless war, a war that we could win,
A brain tumor in your smartphone, an entitlement check
(Will you please check on my entitlement?),
Waiting for the bank-hack, the backtrack, the take,
Waiting for a calabash, the calaboose, an acquisition,
An accusation, resuscitation from a total stranger,
Waiting for the finish line to explode.

Heaven Is a Heavy House:
Axe, Drawknife, Auger, Crosscut Saw

You fell the trees,
You limb them, peel them,
And skid them out.
You raise a heavy house
With heavy rooms,
A heavy loft.

A heavy wet snow
Falls in May,
Snows you in
For five days.

That snow makes new grass heavy,
And heavy with flowers.
There is a heaven
And you are alone in it—
Not even a voice
To talk to yourself in—

Just swerving memories
Of hope and fear
So lethally ephemeral—
A girl playing guitar
And horses in the yard.
You wait for the horse

That comes to your gate
With a bullet hole in his forehead.
He doesn't want anything.

He stares at you,
Then wheels and gallops away,
Leaving you

In the heavy house
You made from life.
A heavy wet snow.
It's like the floor of the sky
Fell out.

The Last Time I Died

—for Richard Borgmann

The mineshaft collapsed behind me
As if coughing me
Out of its ribcage of rotten oak.
It belched black smoke
And hawked me up.
I coughed up
Coal dust and black damp
From my crushed chest
Like the mineshaft
Was inside me.
I wondered what
The broken bone count would be.
I guessed it was more than four.
In the ICU I dreamed on Dilaudid
I buried my face
In the mane of a horse.
Nothing smells better than horses
That have been grazing
On sweet grass in sagebrush.
I woke tied to the bed
With a tube down my throat
Which breathed for me.
I had to assume the room
Smelled of air-conditioning
And hospital sheets.
All I could see
Was the clock on the wall.
It was ten till three in eternity.

Entering the Desert

Sorry, pal,
You're in the desert now,

Nothing you can do
About it.

Don't look for water.
That just complicates matters.

Under the anesthetic sky
The desert doesn't hurt.

The everlasting swoop inside your chest
Is grief, not fear. Get used to it.

It's not the desert's fault.
Despite its name, the desert never

Deserted anyone. Under the anesthetic sky
The desert doesn't hurt.

It welcomes all comers,
But turning back is impossible.

If you venture far enough into the desert,
You come to a place with your name on it.

It seems personal, but it's not.
It's just a name. It was always just a name.

Keep going.
You have no destination.

A Ceremony

My father coughed up a few bats
And that was that.
With a smithy's hammer,
I broke and flattened his gold heraldic ring.
"Hit it again," my sister said,
And I did.
There were three of us.
We stashed the ashes with the ring
In a cairn of black rocks.
My niece piped up,
"Isn't anybody going to say something?"
I looked at my sister,
Who shook her head.
"Nope," I said,
And the three of us walked away.

Convenience Store

After the wreck I hunkered on the floor
Of the Casey's store in Dexter, Iowa.
I'd got my still-scared dog, at least, from out
Of the cornfield where he'd run when we stopped rolling
Over. I'd lost my wallet and didn't know
How long I'd have to wait for a friend to come
One hundred fifty miles in such a storm.
I wasn't bleeding noticeably anymore.
In Carhartt coveralls the locals came.
They knew each other and talked about conditions
As they stood in line with their pops and Copenhagen.
Some glanced at my dog and me and must have wondered.
A woman asked what I was doing there.
She said she had a border collie herself.
She had curly red hair under her baseball cap,
An open, fiftyish, freckled, windburned face.
I told her what had happened and the worst was
I couldn't have rented a motel room even
If there was one in Dexter, Iowa,
Which there was not. She asked me if she could buy
Me something to eat. I said I was okay.
She petted the dog and promised to call the store
In two hours' time to make sure I wasn't there.
She said she'd bring me home with her. This poem,
If that is what it is, is for that woman,
Who will never see these lines and doesn't
Have to, to know exactly who she is.

Long Distance

I know you remember the time I phoned you
From inside a redwood tree.
You answered from behind a waterfall.
You were a woolly caterpillar then.
I know you remember when communications of that sort
Were meaningful. Now we call
From more preposterous locations.
I call you from an unspecified mall.
You answer from inside a preposition,
With a proposal. Highly speculative.
Let's put all of that away.
It didn't get us anywhere.
Call me from inside your own heartbeat.
I'll answer from the green rushes
Of before anything happened.

What It's Like

The trout that twists free
Of the osprey's talons
And falls against all odds into water.
An alpine glacial lake with no other fish,
And no outlet through the moraine.

Arohanui

Small tent in big rain, Rain rivering onto us and under us
Where we perched like a mollusk
On a finback ridge high above
The Whanganui River.
The Flying Fox carried us in its claws—
A coal bucket on a zip line—
Across the river and delivered us
To the Glory Cart
And the Bush Tub
Where we drank wine and simmered
Into the night of that spellbound land.
Arohanui.

The same small tent on a deserted beach
By the Abel Tasman Sea.
A single Brit tramped past
Whistling the "Colonel Bogey March."
Sea kayaks, Zamboni races,
The waterfall that fell
And whipped back up
Like a horse's tail with a rainbow in it,
And never reached the rocks
That it was falling for,
The oddball bird you befriended there
(What was it called?).
My oafish remarks about Dryden,
Sushi on a conveyor belt,
Rope bridge in high wind.
Arohanui.

The plastic tables at Due Ciccioni,
Heart-covered walls of Vicolo del Cinque,
Across the Ponte Sisto with its beggars
And their depressed pets,
Into the City,
Papal vestments for sale in the window
Of the holy clothing outlet,
The woman masturbating
And calling out to God
In front of the Pantheon,
Hades's fingers indenting Persephone's thigh,
All Bernini's women reminding me of you.
Tuesdays and Fridays at L'Archetto,
You at the market buying tangerines
In your new Italian.
The train to Ravenna, Ravenna,
The holy splendor of San Vitale,
Dante's boring tomb,
Neapolitans on the train eating tuna
From a can with their fingers.
Arohanui.

You giving me the finger
At the top of Aspen Highlands
(My life will never be richer),
Saratoga's tepees,
Ocelot-Toledo in the panhandle
Of Nebraska, the girl
Whose life was all mapped out
In layers of scars on her arm,
In the juvenile detention home,
Also in Toledo,

Wacky T-shirts like the one you never wore
From the store called
Liquor Here, Liquor There,
Reading to each other in bed:
Huck Finn, Treasure Island,
The Secret Garden.
Arohanui.

Redwood trees, Sea Lion Caves,
Driving across the desert at night,
You riding Kinky Chick across the canyon
The horse guru shied from,
Staying on one side whispering to himself,
Other horses in distant pastures,
Tails lazily swishing at flies,
You spotting the smolder
An hour after the storm was over,
You running to fetch the shovels
That saved the whole shebang.
You in your enormous straw sun hat,
Walking over the flower-blown hill
To your studio,
Sketchpad under your arm.
Arohanui.

No more.
The last thing we do together
Is disappear to each other
Into the ether called
No more, no more.
Arohanui.

Why I Am like New Zealand

My feet stick out from beneath the sheet,
Pointing to where death thrives.
I am right side up.
I wake between tectonic plates that hurt.
I have five faults, called senses.
My brow is furrowed into alps.
My best volcano thinks
It's high geologic time
To euthanize the sky.
Excuse me while I euthanize the sky.
My fjords ache.
My glaciers hurry.
My spine is a train wreck in a tunnel.
No one survives.
There *is* a bridge to nowhere, and it's mine.
I count on being left alone.
I love the Abel Tasman Sea.
I can't remember my discovery.

About the Author

James Galvin was raised in northern Colorado. He has published
seven previous collections of poetry, most recently *As Is* (Copper
Canyon, 2009). He is also author of the critically acclaimed prose
book *The Meadow* and the novel *Fencing the Sky*. His honors include
a Lila Wallace–Reader's Digest Writers' Award, a Lannan Literary
Award, and fellowships from the Guggenheim Foundation, the
Ingram Merrill Foundation, and the National Endowment for
the Arts. He has a home and some horses outside of Tie Siding,
Wyoming, and is a member of the permanent faculty of the
University of Iowa Writers' Workshop.

Poetry is vital to language and living. Since 1972, Copper Canyon Press has published extraordinary poetry from around the world to engage the imaginations and intellects of readers, writers, booksellers, librarians, teachers, students, and donors.

WE ARE GRATEFUL FOR THE MAJOR SUPPORT PROVIDED BY:

THE PAUL G. ALLEN
FAMILY FOUNDATION

4
CULTURE

Anonymous

Donna and Matt Bellew

John Branch

Diana Broze

Janet and Les Cox

Beroz Ferrell & The Point, LLC

Alan Gartenhaus and Rhoady Lee

Mimi Gardner Gates

Linda Gerrard and Walter Parsons

Gull Industries, Inc.
on behalf of William and Ruth True

Mark Hamilton and Suzie Rapp

Carolyn and Robert Hedin

Steven Myron Holl

Lakeside Industries, Inc.
on behalf of Jeanne Marie Lee

TO LEARN MORE ABOUT UNDERWRITING
COPPER CANYON PRESS TITLES,
PLEASE CALL 360-385-4925 EXT. 103

WE ARE GRATEFUL FOR THE MAJOR SUPPORT PROVIDED BY:

Maureen Lee and Mark Busto

Brice Marden

Ellie Mathews and Carl Youngmann as The North Press

H. Stewart Parker

Penny and Jerry Peabody

John Phillips and Anne O'Donnell

Joseph C. Roberts

Cynthia Lovelace Sears and Frank Buxton

The Seattle Foundation

Kim and Jeff Seely

David and Catherine Eaton Skinner

Dan Waggoner

C.D. Wright and Forrest Gander

Charles and Barbara Wright

The dedicated interns and faithful volunteers of Copper Canyon Press

The Chinese character for poetry is made up of two parts:
"word" and "temple." It also serves as pressmark for
Copper Canyon Press.

The poems are set in Janson.
Printed on archival-quality paper.
Book design and composition by Phil Kovacevich.